7

Reasons why we get

STUCK

How to break Free!

By JoAnn S. Dean
MSW, BCC

FOREWARD

by Pastor Willie Dean, Jr.

Have you ever lost your keys? If so, you know that it immobilizes you. In other words the lost or misplacing of your keys prevents you from moving or operating from that place of normal. One of the definitions for the word key is: "a small piece of metal with incisions cut to fit a particular lock". An adjective for the same word is: "of paramount importance".

In the year 2004, I experienced one of the most difficult seasons in my life. The humiliation of that dreaded word divorce. After several months of agonizing over the loss, I began to pray. I prayed to God the description of the person whom I wanted Him to send me. She had to be a Proverbs 31 woman, with a quiet spirit, supportive and loving. In October of that same year the key that was lost I discovered in my wife, best friend, support system, JoAnn. It was almost scary. But I knew that if I trusted in the Lord that this was the right key. It was the key in the form of my wife JoAnn that would free me from being stuck.

In this wonderful spirit led creation of the *7 Reasons Why We Get Stuck,* know that the Lord is a God of purpose and if this book has found its way to you trust and believe that God's plan is working in your life. Allow this creative and gifted author to take you on a journey on how to break free from being stuck. If you have lost your key, allow this book to cut into the areas of your life to unlock you and set you free. Believe me, she worked for me and now she will work for you. I want to share this dynamic woman with you, the gift that was shared with me, JoAnn Dean.

This book is DEDICATED to my grandmother, Ms. Laura M. Jett. I admire your strength. Thank you for everything!

Table of Contents

Introduction

I was only five years-old. While sitting in my first grade classroom, I was asked to gather my things without any explanation. I was moved to a classroom situated along the kindergarten hallway where I would spend the remainder of the year. I later learned through listening to an adult conversation, that someone had told the school that my age didn't reflect my grade. The tradition in my family was, we went straight to first grade because we were academically prepared. But, in the new classroom, I wasn't prepared for what was to come. I had no idea that from that day onwards, I would stay stuck for a great portion of my life!

While many would say that my life looked great from the outside, I spent many years silently wondering why I revisited feelings of not being good enough or unworthy of opportunities. Sometimes I secretly sabotaged opportunities one after another as they presented themselves before me.

Those feelings that kept me stuck, stemmed from a seed that was sown when I moved from one grade to another without explanation. It was the actions of others that placed me in this vulnerable position. Even though the series of events that took place early on in my life were done with the best intentions in mind, I didn't process them that way. Someone should have explained why I had to move, to remove the blame in my head.

What keeps us stuck is our thinking. But, **Change is possible.** My change began with something I heard: "Change your thinking. Change your life." I sincerely wanted to change. I began that process with what was familiar to me, prayer. I persistently prayed to God for help. I spent time with him daily, praying and reading his word until he revealed why I was stuck. Yes, He really does rewards those who diligently seek him. There are many reasons why we get stuck, stop moving forward and won't ask for or accept help while going through life's experiences. Life happens to each of us, but we are not meant to journey it alone.

As I began my journey to getting UnStuck, I identified *7 areas, which I share in this book*. I am a social worker by trade and I have always believed that the biggest gift I can give to those I come in contact with is one of awareness—helping others to see their options.

My prayer is that this book will help you to identify where you are and inspire you to let go of the reasons why you are staying in that head space and/or physical space. As you read through the pages, be honest with yourself; observe what's happening in and around you. Take notes. Remember who you are and what you have learned along the way, can work for your benefit.

Your success will be based on the next decision you make. You are strong enough to face every challenge while creating the life you want to live.

Don't resist the opportunities these pages will give you. Dive in, interrupt some behavior patterns and create a new story. Don't underestimate the power of YOU!

Let's get started with the 7 Reasons.

Reason #7
Bad Habits

A bad habit is a negative behavior pattern.

Bad habits interrupt your life and prevent you from accomplishing your goals. One of my behavior patterns included self-sabotage. This behavior pattern kept me from trying things that took me outside of my comfort zone, for fear of failure. It also caused me to miss opportunities. What we learn early on tends to inform our perception throughout our lives.

Your healing will come from understanding that there is a perceived, unconscious benefit to negative behaviors. These behaviors are clues that need to be examined. Begin interrupting these behavior patterns by creating a morning routine that will set the tone for your day. My morning routine included prayer, which brought clarity and confidence to my life.

Reason #6
Isolation

The state of being in a place or situation that is separate from others.

According to New York Times, "social isolation is a growing epidemic; one that's increasingly recognized as having dire physical, mental and emotional consequences."

We were not created to do things alone! Face-to-face interactions are valuable. Even though I preferred to be alone, I became active in my church and community. Each conversation I had with someone felt like an added resource. There were many solutions found in our dialogues. Socializing was a great tool for giving myself a confidence boost!

Reason #5
Unforgiveness
"A grudge against someone who has offended you."

Why do we keep a record of wrongs? Maybe it gives us a sense of power.

The essence of forgiveness is the extension of mercy. It's learning to treat others better than they deserve to be treated. Forgiveness is not just about saying words; it's a process in which you make a decision to let go of the negative feelings towards a person. I thought about the many times I needed mercy; maybe I'd unintentionally offended someone. I needed their forgiveness and they needed mine. Once you've chosen to forgive, take action. If you need to, talk to the person who wronged you, write it in a journal or talk about it with someone you trust. You may not feel anything immediately, but you are on your way to emotional freedom.

Reason#4
You're waiting for everything to be perfect
Refusing to accept any standard short of perfection.

According to Brene Brown, a research professor at the University Of Houston Graduate College Of Social Work, perfectionism is not the same thing as striving to be your best. Perfection is not about healthy achievement and growth. People use perfectionism as a shield against the pain of blame, judgment or shame.

I am guilty of spending many years of my life needing everything to be perfect to begin something. I was using perfectionism as my shield.

Because of the negative seed that was planted and took root in me when I was five, I thought I had to be perfect to be accepted. I spent many days feeling anxious and fearing disapproval. I am grateful for the courage I gained to face and work though these challenges. I now serve with excellence, and everything doesn't have to be perfect for me to start anything.

Reason #3
You compare yourself to others
"Comparison is the death of joy." - Mark Twain

YOU ALONE
ARE ENOUGH.
YOU HAVE NOTHING
TO PROVE
TO ANYBODY.
-MAYA ANGELOU

In comparing yourself to others, you decide that you are not as good as them. This is detrimental to your progress. STOP comparing yourself with others and focus on how you can become the best version of you. Comparison is an act of viciousness against yourself. And it is an insult to your creator.

Decide that the only person you have to compete with, is yourself. Aim to be better than you were yesterday. Define what success looks like for you, focus on what you do well, and set a plan in motion. Then celebrate yourself!

Reason #2
Lack of Self-Awareness

Self-awareness is defined as having a clear perception of your personality, including strengths, weaknesses, thoughts, beliefs, motivations and emotions. Self-awareness allows you to understand other people and how they perceive you, your attitude and your responses to them.

There is a place where we fit perfectly, and it is our responsibility to discover it. Ask for help if you need to, but by all means spend time getting to know who you are. I asked God for help. I attended workshops, trainings and I read books and articles that helped me to understand my value. Who I am, really does matters, and the world deserves to benefit from it. That is why I share my life experiences.

Our *thoughts and beliefs* determine how we feel, and this directs our behavior and actions toward ourselves and others. When I lacked self-awareness, I operated beneath my value, entertaining negative thoughts and accepting only the things inside of my comfort zone.

Knowing who you are, shifts the ground beneath you; empowering you; attracting favorable things and giving you the confidence to walk boldly through open doors to new experiences.

Reason#1
No set GOALS/DREAMS

Webster states that a GOAL is what one intends to accomplish or attain.

Not having set goals or a dream meant that I had no target to aim for or work towards. Setting goals helped me to take control of my life. They pulled me out of bed in the morning.

Without goals, you live passively, following the plans of others. Goals give you focus, motivation and accountability. Setting goals stretches you and takes you out of your comfort zone. Forward movement keeps you hopeful, and experiencing progress helps you to feel good about yourself and reminds you of your worth.

Now that I have shared with you how I got stuck and the 7 areas that I identified and worked through to achieve my success, I would like to offer you a plan to take your power back.

Let's start this journey by being real with yourself and the status of your heart as a result of being stuck. Life happens to all of us—the question is, how will we respond to it?

What has caused you to feel stuck?

- Daddy issues
- Missed opportunities
- Feelings of rejection
- An unhealthy environment
- Loss of a loved one
- An illness

WHERE ARE YOU NOW? What are you feeling?

Has your thinking become hazardous to your healing? To heal we must be willing to confront what makes us uncomfortable.

Take note:

_____

_____

_____

_____

_____

_____

The Power of Your Decision!

A decision is the bridge between your thoughts and your actions. Our decisions are influenced by many things: Our values, our environment, what others think, etc. Not making a decision is also making a decision. If you are aware of the consequences, it only make sense for you to make decisions that support your goals.

By taking responsibility for your decisions, you have more control over the outcome. Decision-making is also connected to setting goals. When we set goals, we agree to follow a set of steps to achieve that goal. Once you understand that making a decision is an agreement, you will gain more clarity about your decision-making, which increases your success rate.

BREAKING FREE!

I DARE you to.....

We need each other!

1) **Join something that matters to you and then act like it matters.**
- Show up
- Be present
- Use your voice

2). **Observe**
- What do you need by way of resources?
- What's already working?
- Who's doing what you desire to do?

3). Analyze Everything – Potential Obstacles
- How committed are you to change?
- Who or what could get in your way?
- What price are you paying to remain the same?
- Everything does not have to be perfect to start.

4). Get Moving - Go dancing, exercise and play
- Movement improves your mood
- Movement boost your energy
- Exercise promotes better sleep
- Physical activity is a great way to have fun, meet new people and feel better!

5). Change things - Don't be a creature of habit.
- It forces your brain to pay attention
- Taking a new route may also help you to break behavior patterns if you don't stop at the usual places along the way

6). Focus on one thing at a time

- This helps you to be present for that experience
- Carve out blocks of time
- Unplug at a designated time each day
- Enjoy where you are

7). Time with God

- It gives you strength
- It fulfills the heart like nothing else can
- Seeking him at the beginning of your day gives you direction
- Worship washes away your worry
- Worship expresses your gratitude

WORSHIP is trusting God enough to fully let him into your life, which gives him access to places you didn't even know existed. We all have a heart condition to some degree, but we can be transformed by his presence.

I encourage you to spend time worshipping God. Budget your time and choose to put him first—I promise you will leave your quiet place experiencing his peace, no matter what's going on around you.

Relationship releases you to worship. Get to know God in a more intimate way. Believe that you are surrounded by LOVED and you are READY!

Reflections

_____

_____

_____

_____

_____

_____

_____

_____

_____

_____

_____

_____

Personal Goal Contract

I _____, am setting

goals to help myself reformulate the following

habit(s)/behavior(s):

_____

_____.

I agree to adhere to these life style changes that are

designed to meet my personal/professional/

spiritual needs. I will obligate myself to

_____hours of the day toward the

intended goal to increase my overall level of

personal satisfaction.

I make this personal goal contract to achieve

_____

_____ .

My incentive will be_____,

which will be rewarded each day/week that I fulfill
my personal contract and come closer to achieving
my goal(s).

Upon attainment of my goal, I plan to reward
myself by _____

_____ .

Signed _____ Date _____

Witness _____ Date _____

How to set your Goals

Of course, change isn't always easy. The first few days will require effort on your part, especially in terms of commitment and discipline. But if you are going to improve your life, then surely it will be worth it.

- ❖ Your goal should be *Specific* - What exactly would you like to achieve?
- ❖ It should be *Measurable* - How will you know you've accomplished it?
- ❖ It should be *Attainable & Realistic* - It must represent an objective which you are both *willing* and *able* to work toward.
- ❖ Finally, your goal should have a *Timeline*. Give it a date!

Example of a goal: I will lose 15lbs over the next three months.

- I will walk three days every week for thirty minutes each day.
- I will drink water instead of soda every day this week.
- I will grocery shop and meal prep on Sundays to plan my meals each week.
- I will weigh in on Monday mornings to track my progress.

My Goal _____

_____

_____

Steps:

       1. _____

          _____

          _____

       2. _____

          _____

          _____

       3. _____

          _____

          _____

Additional Notes

_____

_____

_____

_____

_____

_____

_____

TAKE ACTION!

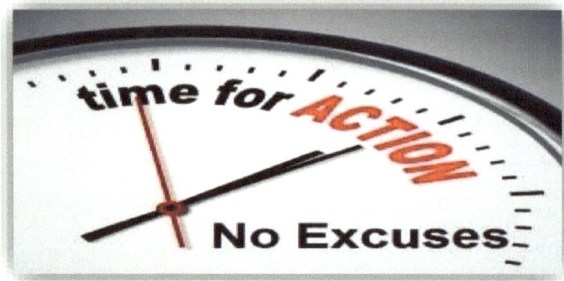

Let's GO:

- Start small
- Ask for help
- Be accountable to yourself
- Get an accountability partner
- Lose the expectation of how things should be
- Work backwards from your vision
- And Celebrate every WIN!

To be yourself in a world that is constantly trying to make you something else is the greatest accomplishment."

- Ralph Waldo Emerson

Lady JoAnn Dean is an Author, Speaker, Mentor and Board-Certified Personal Life Coach. JoAnn has been helping others to help themselves for over twenty years! She is a graduate of Southern University at New Orleans, where she obtained both a Bachelors and Master's Degree in Social Work. She is an alumni of DeVos Urban Leadership Initiative and Life Purpose Institute.

JoAnn is the Founder of **The JD Experience, LLC**—the place where possibilities are awakened and dreams are directed through Personal Life Coaching & Sister Circle Retreat Seminars! JoAnn realized that there was a need for a place where women could feel safe and celebrated while refueling for their journey; gaining clarity and finding peace to live a life more fulfilled without judgment as they continue to serve their families and communities.

JoAnn and her husband Pastor Willie Dean Jr. have been married for eight years and see life as an adventure together.

For I know the plans I have for you," declares the LORD, "plans to prosper you and not to harm you, plans to give you hope and a future.   Jeremiah 29:11

Begin your journey with the understanding that God has a plan for your life. Trust His process. God called all of us to do something different, because we are a special gift to the world. What's your talent/gift? Are you sharing it? If not, what's holding you back?

If you need help with getting clear about who you are and what's important to you, I invite you to visit JoAnn's website at www.joanndean.com or email at inspiredbyjoann@gmail.com to sign up for a **FREE** coaching consult. She will support you on your journey to getting UnStuck.

Putting you first on this journey, doesn't just affect you but the things and those you love as well. Go ahead, give it a try!

Love & Peace

www.ingramcontent.com/pod-product-compliance
Lightning Source LLC
Chambersburg PA
CBHW041808040426
42449CB00001B/11